MEN DON'T ALWAYS LIE

SOMETIMES WOMEN DON'T LISTEN

STOP BREAKING YOUR OWN HEART

NICOLE HARRELL-KELLY

ISBN-13: 978-1535248877
ISBN-10: 1535248874

Book Design by Michael T. Henderson

Acknowledgments

I want to first thank God for giving me this vision and the fortitude to see it through. I thank my children Malik, Jordan and Nija for being understanding for the countless nights they endured me yelling quiet down, I am writing. Thank you for understanding all the nights I ordered take out because I was too tired to cook after writing and edits took up my time. Most importantly I want to thank you for always loving me no matter how hard things got.

A huge thanks to the men who took time out of your schedules to allow me to interview you. I appreciate your openness and honesty. Thanks for keeping it Trill (SMILE!)

Thanks to Michael T. Henderson for designing the perfect cover. You have an amazing eye!

I thank my niece Kali and sister-in-law Marcia for encouraging me to write this book when the flame was first ignited, before pen ever went to paper. I thank my siblings, Andrew, Earl, Angela, Clara, Theaquiata, Irene, Lois and Tina, you all played a crucial part in contributing to the woman I am now. I would be remiss if I did not give a special thanks to my sister Lois for her support in this project. I was going through quite a rough time and ready to give up. I went to my mailbox and noticed an unexpected package with a journal, a note card and $20 that said "Nic this is for the first copy." She had some very inspiring words, but what I remember the most is that she said she believed in me and that I could do it. I had just sold a book, so I guess I had better publish one. God was the only one who knew how much I thought about quitting, and he sent her message to me right on time. But for God!

I appreciate you all and extend a huge thanks to you my audience. Enjoy!

This book is dedicated to

The loving memory of my parents,

Lee and Hilda Harrell

If you were here all I could say is thank you for always telling me I could do anything I put my mind to. I now know exactly what you meant. I love you both. R.I.H.

and to

My children,

Malik Rashad, Jordan Nicholas and Nija Gabrielle

May this book serve as a reminder that no matter how hard the struggle is; never lose faith. Keep your head held high there is a light at the end of the tunnel. I love you all so much. You are my world!

"DON'T BE PUSHED BY YOUR PROBLEMS.
BE LED BY YOUR DREAMS"
~RALPH WALDO EMERSON~

Contents

Introduction

Women if you are tired of going through heartbreak after heartbreak, and you are ready to get out of your own way, ready to admit the truth to yourself about your relationship or lack thereof, then this book is for you.

Here I was over 40, divorced and a single mother of 3, I had enough. I was ready for a serious relationship and I needed to know why I had not been in a real relationship in years. I did some soul searching and lots of journaling. That journaling caused me to pull out old notebooks I had filled with entries from years ago. I hit the jackpot and found and accepted the true meaning behind my heartbreak, my choices!

If you are honest with yourself, you probably blame or have blamed a lot of your relationship fails on the men in your life. Now it is time to face the truth; they are not always to blame. Everyone knows that men do in fact lie sometimes. In fact, I am sure everyone has lied on one occasion or another. Whether it is the small white lie or the big, hairy, ugly, and stinky lie about what is going on in your life.

My intent is to get through to women that the basis of finding love in your life is to first find love in yourself.

Without knowing who you are and understanding where you have been, you cannot cultivate your future.

In a relationship men and women should strive to be honest with each other. Sometimes when given honesty, you may have chosen not to believe it. If you look closely at the situation as it presented itself, you just might notice that men were not always lying to you. Men are usually pretty direct in telling women what they want and or do not want. If a man tells you that he is not ready for or does not want a relationship with you, regardless of the reason, save yourself the drama and keep it moving. When a man tells you that he does not want children, believe him! Do not have kids with him, expecting him to do right by them. When you do those things, you are setting yourself up for failure. Save your heart and do not try to force something that is not there. A lot of times, you may not trust your own judgment or might not listen to those people who care about you the most. Sometimes, you may not even listen to the man in the relationship.

The things I reveal in this book are because I am deeply motivated to see you succeed in relationships and learn from my and your own mistakes. My words are meant to be as honest and informative as possible and to help you discover that life is truly about the choices you make each day. The choices you make today shape your tomorrow.

You have to love yourselves enough to know how and when to avoid creating a bad relationship as well as acknowledging when it is time to end a relationship. Stop holding on to that dying or dead relationship well after you know that a particular man is not a good fit for you. I am not saying leave at the first disagreement, every relationship has problems. When you are consistently unhappy, have expressed your feelings to him and have attempted to make the relationship work, and it does not, move on. It is like trying to fit square pegs into round holes, it is improbable. I will not say impossible, because with a lot of pushing and discomfort it may happen; but how happy will you be?

Nicole Harrell-Kelly

July 2016

Chapter 1

What Are You Attracting?

Who wakes up in the morning, saying I want to break my own heart? I would guess not too many of you. Why do you do it? You do it innocently enough without even realizing it. You enter a relationship knowing full well that the man has already told you what he wants from you, does not want from you, expects from you, and more importantly what he is willing to give you.

When you do not listen to that inner voice and you go against your own intuition, knowing that you have been given the information to choose wisely, you set yourself up for heartbreak. With the many horror stories I have endured, my goal is to help other women see just how we hurt ourselves, and to stop these behaviors.

Why do you enter or continue toxic relationships knowing they are not good for you? You have likely convinced yourself that you can change a man or maybe you just do not believe that there is anything better for you.

Let me start by saying:

1. YOU CANNOT CHANGE A MAN!

and

2. YOU ARE WORTHY!

You are valuable and you deserve to have your own man. You deserve to be in a happy, healthy and enjoyable relationship. YES, you!

People can only treat you how you allow them to treat you. You get to set the standard for how you are treated. You cannot control how a man treats you, but YOU get to decide if you will stick around if he mistreats you. You must start to believe these men and begin to know yourself better. You have to know better than to just accept any attention a man throws your way just to have a resemblance of a relationship.

Until you are honest with yourself about what you really want from a man you are not going to get it. I had been a single mother for so long that my battle cry used to be "what do I need a man for?" "I can do it myself." I pretended to be the epitome of a strong woman when in reality I was just afraid to admit that I wanted and needed a strong stable relationship with a man. It felt less scary to say I did not want him in case he never showed up than to admit that I longed to have a man. I felt weak admitting that I wanted to come home to a man to hug me, kiss me, cuddle with me and tell me he loves me. I longed for adult interactions and want to have my man there to ask about my day and share about his. I want to be in a partnership with my man where he and I can laugh and talk and just enjoy being together. I want a man who appreciates that I will always have his back as long as he treats me with love and respect. At the time I felt that if I admitted that it made me weak. I stopped being afraid to admit it when I learned that I could not get the relationship I wanted because I had built this wall of resistance. If I continued saying that I did not want a relationship, then I would only attract men who were not willing to be in one with me. That is exactly what I attracted. Men looking for a relationship certainly were not going to be attracted to the vibe I was giving off. The guys I dated who said they were not ready for a relationship fit in direct correlation with the vibe that I emitted and what I had said I wanted time and time again. I attracted successful, attractive and interesting men. In some cases there would be one date, other cases a few weeks, several months or a year. Neither I nor they were truly ready for a real relationship and that is why we attracted each other. We may have had different reasons but the attraction point remained the same, no commitment. None of them were looking for a real relationship. I got frustrated when I could not figure out what was wrong with them. In my mind I consider myself attractive, fun, outgoing, interesting, and a good catch. Then I started to hear myself think one day and everything was about how I did not need a man. What good man wants a woman who does not need or want him? I was repelling men like OFF is supposed to repel bugs. I was attracting what I was, not what I wanted. A couple of these men were the mirror image of myself. I had been in messed up relationships and pretty much bore the responsibility of taking care of my children on my own. These men I attracted were single fathers with custody of their kids who had experienced equally painful relationships with the women they had been involved with. I quickly learned that men can go through just as much as women do to find a good relationship.

That is when I decided it was time to learn from my past and get inside the male mind and find out what I could do differently to have better relationships with men. I felt compelled to share with you all what I learned and suspected all along and that is men do not always lie, sometimes women just do not listen.

I am now ready and will do and learn as much as I can about myself and relationships to manifest my man, my husband into my life. You must learn and believe in your true value of self and realize that it is better to be alone than to settle for just anyone.

If you dig deep, you know what you want. You may pretend not to know because you fear you cannot accomplish it, but; DIG DEEP ...You want what you want, you have certain non-negotiables that you look for in a man, and you have chosen those qualities for a reason. Your expectations are not too high. You must believe in it for yourself and go after what you want in order to make you happy. When you are happy, you will not settle for someone just being a part of your life if he is not enhancing it.

Once you do have a good man, there is nothing wrong or weak about showing him that you appreciate him and love him. Men need to know this just as much as women, but they are not always going to tell you that.

Once I was honest with myself, I acknowledged that I do want that one person that I can love who will love me back and who will understand me and support my dreams. I think deep down that is what most people want and are just too afraid to admit it.

"Your thoughts are the architects of your destiny."

~David O. McKay~

Chapter 2

I Asked; They Answered
Questions Posed to Men

This book contains a compilation of men's answers to questions geared to help women understand how to stop breaking our own hearts. There will be some real life relationship examples from my experiences that opened my eyes to realize that what these men were saying is true. One thing is certain they were not shy in expressing how women can help build good relationships with them.

1. **What are the top three relationship killers?**

- Lack of effective communication
- Infidelity
- Lying

I often hear women say that all men are concerned about is sex, however, when asked about the top three relationship killers, surprisingly not a single man mentioned sex. It turns out that men are very much concerned about having open and effective communication with their woman. The number one relationship killer mentioned by the men I spoke with was lack of open communication, followed by a close second infidelity. Lying also topped the charts as the third highest cause of relationship problems. Of course you know that lying leads to a lack of trust and if you cannot have a trusting relationship, there really is no relationship. Men much like women want a partner that they can effectively communicate with, who will be honest and loyal. At the end of the day, when the sex is gone if you have nothing in common what is left.

One man was very direct in his response and stated that "you cannot fuck or suck a man into feelings" and that women need to stop thinking that the "split between her legs is any better than the next woman." I felt that his comment was worth mentioning because I have heard so many women comment how they think they can get a man through sex. His comment may be blunt, nonetheless it is obviously truthful and a lot of women need to realize this fact.

Communication means listening to what the man is saying he wants and or does not want as well as being honest about what you are truly after and not trying to change one another. One man expressed his frustration in women agreeing to one type of a relationship and then trying to manipulate something more. If a man shows you and tells you where you stand with him, and you refuse to listen and believe it, you are practicing ineffective communication skills. When you swear that you can change him and that he only has to get to know you, you are not practicing good communication skills. Communication is more than just talking, you also have to listen. What you have to realize is that it does not matter how much a man knows you, when he knows himself and has determined that you are not the one, he is not going to commit to you. Communication must be clear and honest on both ends, otherwise, this is where things will usually start to heat up and tempers flare. You cannot make a man feel any way about you that he does not choose to. Here is when, as my mom used to say you learn that "a hard head makes for a soft behind". You chose not to listen and now come the consequences of your actions. Ladies you can be fabulous, super model sexy with a banging body or just a regular "plain Jane" and it will not mean anything to that man who does not want you. You can have money, a great personality, heck you can be the most wonderful woman he knows, but unless that man sees it for himself that he is ready to commit to *you*, you are just spinning your wheels. You are going nowhere fast. Every man I interviewed had one common response and that is you cannot change a man. He will either verbally communicate how he feels or does not feel about you or his actions will speak very loudly.

2. **How important is openness and honesty in a successful relationship?**

The majority of those interviewed expressed that openness and honesty are the key building blocks to a successful relationship. It was said that without that important foundation that a woman should not expect an opportunity for growth. This answer should come as no surprise since lying was one of the top three relationship killers.

The next question was broken into two parts after an interviewee pointed out that the original question, "how important is communication in an intimate relationship?" needed clarification. He wanted to make it clear that you can be "intimate" with just about anyone regardless of being in a committed relationship. Please pay attention to the differences between the answers to these questions when talking to a man.

3. How important is communication
a) In an intimate relationship?

You have to make sure that you are both on the same page. The conversation likely ends after, "I like you, I dig you, I want to hang out and kick it with you, but I am not really looking for anything serious." In that aspect communication is important because you will need to know that if you choose to have sex with this man that is likely all it will be. You are not in a committed, exclusive relationship so you are leaving yourself open to the possibility of being one of many women who are all made to feel special at the moment. Once you get past the initial phases of why you are both there it is rare that there will be much more relationship talk after that.

b) In a committed relationship?

Communication is of the utmost importance just as honesty is. You have to be able to communicate effectively with your partner. There has to be a balance where you and your partner are pretty much equally yoked, otherwise your communication skills will be like oil and water and will never mix. There must be a point where one of the two is willing to put the relationship above their differences and not jump down one another's throat, putting differences aside and talking the issue out.

4. **Do you believe more relationships are destroyed from lack of honest communication or lack of sex?**

    The majority of the men I spoke with indicated that lack of honest communication is more important than the lack of sex. As one man put it, since communication is one of the building blocks for a relationship, he has to know what he is getting into when deciding if a woman is for him. Most men interviewed are aware that the majority of the time when a woman shuts down on sex, it is because her defenses have been triggered because of something that the man has done or that she believes he has done. They feel like women jump to conclusions rather than sitting down and airing out their differences to get clarification of the situation at hand. Most men seem to think that if you have effective communication everything else just falls into place.

5. **What is your take on women pursuing men?**

    A good portion of the men seem to agree that it is okay for women to pursue men if they are interested. As one man stated no one likes rejection, but men run the risk of being rejected daily. One man advised that women should not to be discouraged if it does not work out and to not let it stop you from trying again. It was mentioned that men like to know that they are wanted and desired just as women do. One man put it like this, "If there is a man who really does it for you, do not to be afraid to go for it, it is 2016 not 1947." He stated, that it is okay for people to pursue people. He does believe there should still be clear delineations between male and female roles, but that two people expressing interest in one another is perfectly ok.

6. **Have you ever had a relationship end due to lack of forgiveness?**

    While infidelity did not come in as the number one reason for relationship failure, it did get mentioned as the most unforgivable indiscretion in a relationship. While most men agreed that they can forgive a woman for things like lying, punctuality and reliability to a small degree, the one thing that was almost unanimously agreed upon was that they could not under any circumstances forgive a woman for cheating on them. I did not find this surprising, however I did find it interesting that most of these same men openly admitted to cheating on the women they have been with on a consistent basis. Each of them got very emotional at the idea of a woman cheating on them. Although I am sure this does not come as a surprise that men loathe the idea of a woman they are intimate with being with someone else. One man went as far as saying about himself, "I could never marry me." At first, I laughed until he explained that what he meant was simply that there was no way that he would marry a woman who led a lifestyle similar to his. He posed the question "who wants to marry someone's bonafide hoe?" Ladies this man was very clear and went as far as stating "no man wants to wed the popular slut." It should not come as a surprise that a lot of men do feel this way, regardless of how they live. If you are looking for that knight and shining armor to come and swoop you up, it is not likely to happen while you are hopping from bed to bed.

Take time between relationships and get to know yourself because otherwise you will consistently have the same relationship with different men.

7. **Do you believe that men in this day and age are less likely to marry than generations before?**

I learned that quite a few men do still believe in the covenant of marriage and acknowledge it as a Godly sacrament. Some men while they are for marriage did point out that with sex being so prevalent and with social media and dating sites readily accessible that it is much more likely that they will date much more before settling down. They feel that there are too many options to get married right away and be with one person who may not be the one. With that said a few did mention that when a good woman comes around they would be willing to drop everything to make it work. One man said "We all should know that marriage is what you make it and everyday will not be perfect but I am ready for the challenge and when I find that one woman that supports and encourages me, I am not letting her go"

With that said ladies if you are looking for marriage, it is time to bring your A-Game or go home. Do not get too attached to a man too soon because while your falling in love, he may be falling out of like and looking to other options. Women should learn to better control emotions and be willing to explore other options as well. I am not saying to sleep with multiple men, I am saying get to know other men and befriend them. No man who is not trying to claim you as his woman should be a factor that prevents you from meeting and dating other men. This gives you the option to choose.

I had a man tell me "I chose you" in my mind I was thinking "that's cool, but I also chose you". Everyone has options and never let a man make you believe that he is your only option. If he is not treating you as a priority, you have every right to leave. You may notice a trend in this book and that is good, I want you to see the point. This book is not out to bash men. Men can say or do whatever they choose, just as you can, but here is the kicker, will you CHOOSE to ALLOW him to treat you any way he wants even if you disapprove? The theme of this book is accountability. You absolutely must take responsibility for your own actions.

When you do something good you are quick to take the credit, so it is time to start taking ownership of your mishaps as well, it is the only way to learn from them. If you do not then you are refusing to grow. This cannot be so if you want to have positive and productive relationships.

"The best relationship is the one in which your love for each other exceeds your need for each other."
~Dalai Lama~

Chapter 3

The Truth Will Set You Free

There are two important things to consider when developing a relationship:

1. ***Are you happy?***
2. ***Is your partner happy?***

If a man says he does not want to be with you, believe him! How many times have you jokingly told a man who you were interested in that you did not want him? I am going to go out on a limb here and say that you probably have not. Conversely if you have a man tell you that he wants to be with you and you are not interested in him I am willing to bet that you would let him know as much. You owe it to yourself and that man to look inside yourself and decide if you want him in your life. Men have feelings also and can be hurt just as women. If you want men to be honest and upfront with you, you have to give them the same respect. I came across men whose stories resembled my own, stories of pain, heartache, cheating and being left to raise their children alone. Women do not have the market cornered on pain.

Life is not a game or a fairy tale and sometimes feelings will get hurt. I hear women talk about how men string them along and how they get upset because the relationship did not move forward in the way they had hoped it would. Keep it real though, how many men out there could say that women have strung them along also? You may realize that a particular man is not the one for you, but you want to hang on to him because right now he seems to be the best prospect. Is that fair to him? If you answered yes, then do not complain when a man does it to you. If you answered no, then you have been paying attention. No doubt men and women are different, however if we listen to one another things would be much less complicated. You cannot understand anything or anyone that you choose to not pay attention to.

How many times have you played along with a man who says he does not want a relationship? You secretly thought to yourself how you are going to "put it on him", cook for him, clean for him, or whatever else you may do to convince him to choose you. That is not being honest. Six months down the line when you are not in a relationship with that man, you are pissed at him for "playing with your emotions". You played with your own emotions because you thought you were slick. The reality is you were giving him what he wanted and you were not being honest about what you wanted. He had told you what he wanted and you agreed, just to get your foot in the door. You complain that you cannot understand why he does not want a relationship with you after all you have done for him. This behavior is what leads men to think women are crazy! He is ready to call the looney bin on you since he has been straight up from the beginning and now you are mad that he is not doing what you wanted him to.

Ladies I am only trying to help you learn from my own mistakes. Life has a way to teach you the same lesson over and over until you finally get it. Trust me when I tell you I learned it well after many years and several failed relationships. I used to blame men all the time for my relationship failures. I had so many pity parties and woe is me moments that I could have been the poster child for failed relationships. This book speaks about a few relationships, but the one that really woke me up and inspired the book was the relationship or situation-ship in which I fell in love with a man who I should not have for one very specific and obvious reason, he had someone else.

This man and I talked about relationships some time later, and he like the other men interviewed, said the same thing - when a man tells you something, you need to believe him. When a man informs you of what he wants or does not want, it is done specifically to let you know not to get your feelings involved. If what he wants does not line up with what you want or vice versa, keep it moving. He is giving you a choice! No one is going to be able to protect your heart better than you do. Choose wisely!

He may not come out with the exact words "hey do not get your feelings in this." He will likely say something similar to "I have a friend", "I have someone I kick it with", "I am not looking for a relationship", "You are a good friend, but…," or "I can't commit", etc. You get the picture. When you notice what he wants and what you want do not line up, do not pick at him to appease you. Know that he has a right to want something different than you and that you have the right to choose another man.

Some women are quick to say that a man used her or played her. You can only be played or used when you are uninformed about the situation. When a man comes out of his mouth and tells you full on what his situation is or shows you who he is, you are not being used, you are not being abused, and you are not being played. You have been given a choice. If you made the conscious decision to dive into that situation knowing that both your values did not line up and now you are in the deep end sinking, it is nobody's fault but your own. Do not try to throw the blame on anyone else and do not try to play the victim. You are a grown woman and you made your choices, now it is time to face the consequences. Get up, pull on your big girl panties and learn from your last lesson. Take enough pride in yourself and love yourself enough to get back on the market and this time make better choices. If you want love, commitment, and or a family, do not settle for the man who has someone else, the one who cannot commit, the one who does not want children, do not even settle for the one who says "I am not ready now." Leave him alone too, and be with someone you are interested in who is ready now. If you are available and Mr. Not Ready comes back around, you will be in the position to decide if he is still someone you are interested in.

I do not care how fine he is, how successful he is, how big his *package* is, I do not care about any of that. I care about your well-being. I care about you not getting hurt. If you go out there and hurt yourself getting involved with someone else's man, or kicking it with the man who does not want a relationship right now or anything else that tells you that he does not want you, then you have made the choice to play his game and it is not his fault. It is yours!

You have to stop playing victim. Listen for the man who says something like "yes I want to see where this goes with you" or "I got your back let's do this." Women are strong and independent in so many areas of our lives, so we cannot continue to act like helpless prey in our relationships. It does not serve you well, and if you have children, it does not serve them well to see a weakened version of a woman. Playing the victim only sets you up for failure because when you view yourself as a victim, you will never acknowledge your role in your failed relationships. This can cause you to repeat the same relationship over and over with different men. Until you look inward at what is going on with you, you will continue to have one poor relationship after another.

Everyone has an inner voice that nudges them when something is right or not right. When you get quiet enough to hear that voice and stop shutting it down because you do not like what it is saying, you will be in a much better position to choose to have healthy and happy relationships.

Loyalty

Most little girls were trained to be loyal and date one guy at a time and to claim him as your boyfriend. *Has he claimed you?* When some females start to date someone new, they have not communicated the desire to be the girlfriend or his woman. They may think it is too soon to express what they want but somehow once they have sex they assume that they are magically a couple, and oh she better not see *her* man with someone else.

> ➤ *Does he know that he is your man?*

Ladies I hate to break it to you, but the majority of men do not instantly assume a relationship with you because of sex. Unless you actually communicate your desire to him and get his confirmation that you are in a relationship, you probably are not. Sex does not seal the deal for you. I do not care if you see each other every day, and have sex twice on Sunday. You two could spend romantic nights together and he may still just think of you as that really cool girl. Do not assume that you are a couple until the two of you have communicated and decided together that you are in a relationship.

Imagine how you would feel if you saw that man you think you are in a relationship with out on a date with another woman. He is treating her the same way he treats you. I am going to guess you do not want to envision that. You thought you were special. Right?

Scenarios like that are why you have to clarify where you stand with a man as soon as possible. If you do not ask certain questions you may not get very important information. I have learned through experience that about 80-90% of the time when I have asked a man a question, I have gotten an honest answer. You may not like the response that you get, it may not be what you want to hear nevertheless you cannot ignore it. When you choose to ignore the truth, you set yourself up for failure. "The truth shall set you free" John 8:32, is not just some cute biblical verse. When applied it is very true, when you ask a question and are lied to you are not free to choose wisely, you have been ill informed. When you know the truth of any situation, you can freely choose whether or not you want to be a part of it based on the information received. When you refuse to ask questions because you are afraid of the replies you go in blind and run a greater risk of being hurt. When you assume, without asking any questions, you give the guy the option to say those lines that really piss us women off, things like, "We never agreed to be exclusive" or "When did we decide we were in a committed relationship." These simple comments can cut like a knife, especially if you really thought you were the only one. Once you get out of your feelings you will recognize these phrases for what they really are, simple truths. If you never take the time to define what you have, you cannot assume it is a relationship, and there is nothing for you to be mad about. I often hear people say that actions speak louder than words, while this may have some truth to it, I say clarify until the actions and words are in alignment with each other. Anything else leaves room for mixed messages and confusion.

Ladies I want you to understand this, if you are in a "relationship" make sure that it is not one-sided. Women tend to be led more by emotions and see what is wanted rather than what is actually going on. Excitement kicks in when the man you are interested in asks you out. Then he asks you out again and you are all like "Ooh I think he likes me." A few weeks later you have told everybody "he could be the one." After a couple of months your new mantra is "I am in love." You are on cloud 9 and life is sunshine and rainbows because you are in love. You have opened yourself up fully to this man and you have not stopped to ask or looked to see if he has opened himself up to you in the same way. You give your all and you become loyal and exclusive to him, you never think to ask if he wants an exclusive relationship because you assume you are so great, how could he not. STOP assuming and START asking! When you finally ask and he tells you he is not exclusive with you, or maybe he is exclusive but does not want to move the relationship forward, you get your heart broken. What happens then? You convince yourself that he broke your heart, you believe he did you wrong, he is no good, and the reality is he did not do anything to you.

You did not ask the proper questions, for example;
You did not ask:

1. *Are you single?*
2. *Am I the only woman that you are seeing?*
3. *What type of a relationship are you looking for with me?*
4. *Is this just sex?*

You may feel a little awkward or embarrassed to ask these questions, but you have to be specific. Your heart is on the line. If you do not ask now you will wonder later and that will bring a weird and awkward vibe to the relationship. He will pick up on it and you may not necessarily be able to explain how you feel but your actions will have changed and that is usually where things get sticky. With so much talk about "Friends with Benefits" you need to know as soon as possible if he sees you as relationship material, or if you have been categorized as a FWB. You have to be big enough and strong enough to dig deeper and ask "where do you see this going?"

There are too many ways to play on words that will result in you not getting what you want. I had a man tell me in my younger years, "Baby, no it's not just about sex", and so I just knew that we were relationship bound. Wrong! We were not just sex, we talked on the phone regularly, texted each other often, and saw each other frequently, including our birthdays and holidays. I was taking college courses and still found time to help him with his homework. Sounds a little like a relationship, right? Except for the fact that we always hung out at his house or mine and had no real commitment. He had no intention of growing a relationship with me. He had been twice divorced and had said that he did not want a relationship. After several months of seeing each other, I thought he had changed his mind. Psych! The joke was on me! He had no desire to commit to me. We had more than just sex, but we lacked commitment and connection. We lacked laughter and fun, we were not headed anywhere.

Unless you specifically ask what your relationship is AND believe him when he tells you, you could find yourself somewhere between any of the scenarios below and many more.

- *It's not just sex– you are also a friend*
- *It's not just sex– I like your company*
- *It's more than sex – you are easy to talk to*
- *It's not only about the sex – but I do not see a future with you*

Make sure that whatever scenario he has planned that you are aware of it. If you agree with it cool, if not bounce. If he just wants sex and that is not what you want, walk away. If you choose to have sex with him, do it because you want to. Do not just give in because you think he will choose you for a relationship. He will not! If he told you it is just sex believe him, he means it. Take him at his word. If you choose to stay after he has disclosed that the two of you want different things, remember one thing, it is not his fault you did not take heed. You cannot force yourself into a man's life and when you try to he loses any respect he had for you because you look desperate.

I have come to learn that men are pretty straight forward about what they want. If he has told you it is not a relationship and that he is not ready, believe him. I know it may be scary to think that you might not hear what you want to him to say; would you rather hear it and know the truth in the beginning or to find out months later that he never cared? Do not give him what he wants in the form of just sex; if you want more, do not waste your time. Go out on dates, meet people, have fun, truly get to know you and trust your own judgment. You have to be knowledgeable enough to recognize that if you know what you want, you cannot be afraid of the answer you receive.

You cannot blame him if he has told you what he wanted, just because you thought you could change his mind. In fact it is just the opposite, you have to know that when a man tells you something it is in your best interest to listen.

Most men are not out to see how many women they can hurt. If he cares enough to be honest, you have to be adult enough to take responsibility for your actions.

Look at it this way, you have a beautiful car that you absolutely love and this car only reaches 60 miles per hour. You are about to enter a race but you find out that your car must go at least 90 miles per hour to even have a chance to win. You love your car nevertheless you know that it is not fast enough. You get every possible modification, and even still, you find out the car is only capable of reaching a maximum speed of 75 miles per hour. Do you keep your current car knowing that it will never afford you the opportunity to win; or do you get a new car that is just as visually appealing and reaches a minimum of 100 miles per hour?

> ➢ **Easy right?**
> **You would get the new car that would give you the best opportunity to win.**

That is the analogy my sister Lois gave me when I communicated to her that I had met a man who possessed almost everything that I wanted in a man, with one exception. He could not commit to me. As much as I loved this man, even with "modifications" it became very clear that if I ever wanted to "win" in a relationship I had to keep my options open for an equally appealing man who was willing to commit to me.

The same is true for relationship endings. If a man tells you it is over, walk away. Too many times you try to fix things that are non-negotiable and they become bigger problems. You think he will change his mind if you do certain things he likes and treat him a certain way. I need you to hear me – a man will not change, unless he wants to. Walk away, or better yet run! You have to fall back, relax and get yourself in order. He may come back, he may not, but you have to let go and focus on your own alignment. If he comes back for another chance – You decide if you want what he is offering based on what he is *showing* you now, not how you *felt* then.

I am taking my time and learning who I am and loving me again. I have learned to love people from a distance when they show me that they do not value me. The one you are meant to be with will manifest when you truly and wholly love yourself and probably when you least expect. It may be someone you know or it may be someone new, but rest assured you and your perfect mate will connect when you are both ready. When you each release resistance and are ready to accept what the other has to offer and give what you both truly want is when the magic will happen.

"Your task is not to seek love, but merely seek and find all the barriers within yourself that you have built against it"

~Rumi~

Chapter 4

Give Me My Space!

This chapter gives insight to the cause of my downward spiral that led to the relationship choices discussed in Chapters 8-11, where I set myself up for heartbreak.

I got my first real boyfriend when I was 17, he had just turned 21. He was an only child from a wealthy family; opposed to me, the eighth of nine children with two parents who worked their butts off to send us to private school and make ends meet. I remember hoping that he would not be one of those egotistical and pretentious men who simply talked about how much he had. A man's wealth, has never impressed me. I would much rather be with a man with a good heart.

I gave this relationship a chance because he seemed to be a genuinely good guy. I found it attractive that he never boasted or bragged about what he had and I loved that he construed confidence and not arrogance and accepted me for who I was. I had gotten my licenses only a few months earlier and had no car at that time. He drove an expensive sports car, and had just bought another brand new car. He insisted that I drive his new car, he said, no girl he dated had to be without a car. That unexpected gesture was cute and also kind of funny to me as a 17 year old kid, but it meant a lot.

While we were dating, I got sick once and this man showed up and showed out. He came to my mother's house with flowers, juice, and soup. He fed me, held my cup while I drank, fluffed my pillows and rubbed my feet. You name it, he handled it. Those things are more important to me than any bank account. Anyone can spend their money, but when a man gives you his time, attention, and shows concern as well that speak volumes.

For my 18th birthday he surprised me with 18 roses delivered to my high school with a beautiful card that told me how much I meant to him. We spent considerable time together both alone as a couple and with each other's friends. I respected the fact that even though he was older, he showed patience and never pressured me for sex. I thought I had hit the jackpot, he was sweet, caring, nice looking, fun, funny, and going to school to be a surgeon. What more could I want? Just before I was about to let him know that I was ready to move the relationship to the next level, things got weird.

I have no idea what happened to him but he snapped. He started to behave in a bizarre way. I later found out that he had been following me all around. The day he showed up in a department store as I browsed the clothes racks was when it all came out. As I was looking through clothes I began to hear a rustling sound. I looked around and saw no one. Then I heard the noise again. I looked up to see garments falling off the racks, but still I saw no one around. I was spooked at that point to be honest. I began to walk towards another department when I heard a screeching sound. I started to move a little faster and looked back to find the rack moving behind me. Now I was dang near running to another section when I noticed him fall through the clothes rack. My initial thought, "this man has officially lost his mind."

When I confronted him about it, he said "Nicole I just love you so much and don't want to lose you." The sad part is I liked him and I had no intention to leave him, until after that of course. I had never indicated I wanted anyone else or wanted out of the relationship. We had not had sex so I know that had not motivated his odd behavior. Everything he had done came so sudden. Still to this day, I could not begin to tell you what brought any of it on. He called and came by several times afterwards until I made it clear that we were through. I could not deal with something like that long term. Why would I? He had no reason to believe that I had done a single thing or that I planned to break up with him.

I learned at a young age that a person's insecurities can cause them to behave in strange ways. Once I got that revelation I had to tell myself I had no obligation to stay with him. No matter how good things were at one point, I had the right to make a different choice regarding the relationship at that point. His actions changed and therefore my reactions changed.

When our freedom is threatened we tend to run far away from the threat. This man had made me run so far that I never looked back. No matter what good qualities were shown previously, I was now forced to look at the overall picture.

Sometimes you have to look deep inside yourself and ask if you want a particular man in your life, and if so why? You have to ask, am I happy in this relationship? You have to decide if the costs outweigh the benefits. In the case above, they did not. He had no reason to distrust me. If he could not trust me to the point that he followed me, what type of life would either of us have together? Even though I was young, I knew enough then to listen to my inner voice and remove myself from unfulfilling relationships that did not feel right.

When I reflected back, I realized that with the exception of my ex-boyfriend following me, my first relationship was everything I wanted. He was handsome, caring, compassionate, fun, and funny, he was also success driven. What I learned though is that I had built a wall of resistance for a long time after our relationship against the type of man I really wanted. I began settling for lesser treatment and lesser quality men for fear that a man who had all the qualities I wanted would be "too good to be true." I never realized that fear had been the cause of many self-sabotaging occurrences in my relationships that followed.

As I looked back I noticed a pattern in myself. When things were going well with a man I liked and he would express what he liked about me or the relationship, it was like a trigger. I unconsciously begin to behave the opposite of what he expressed being attracted to about me. As some of my examples will illustrate, I had extremely low points with men who really were not my type whom I should have walked away from early on. Then there were the relationships with men who were more my type that I would do things out of my character to be in relationship with.

I have since become very aware and conscious of my attitudes and fears. The insecurity and doubt that once controlled me, I have now taken control over. You have to learn yourself in order to have a truly successful relationship with someone else. Once you know and accept who you are it allows you to accept your man for who he is.

"Understanding is the first step to acceptance, and only with acceptance can there be recovery"

~JK Rowling~

Chapter 5

Flip the Script

Before you judge the man on the previous pages too harshly, put the shoe on the other foot. Think about your past relationships. Have you ever found yourself on the other end of the crazy train? Be honest. Has your man ever needed his space, but you refused to give it to him because you thought you would lose him or that there might be someone else?

When you try to grab a man to pull him closer, look back over your past and you will probably see that you pushed him further away. Guess what, men get just as scared as women, if not more so. If the man has ever been hurt, well then be prepared for more caution than usual. If he is not ready for a relationship, respect that. You have two options: move on, or try to force it. If you choose the latter make sure you know whatever you get as a result is your fault and not his. He warned you that he was not ready.

Persistence is one thing, but to doggedly try to invade that man's space is another and it is not attractive. Would you want a man who is not interested in you or that you have to chase to be with? Every cell is screaming that you are not happy, and it feels embarrassing to chase him, but you do it anyway.

You can show interest in a man, but do not give chase. If he shows no interest, move on. Is it worth being with that fine, sexy, popular, athletic, or funny man who refuses to give you what you want or need? If you are constantly in doubt about what you mean to him and always have to wonder, you already know your answer.

When a man wants you he makes sure to let you know it in words and actions. I learned and I am still learning that I can be attracted to a man, but if he is not interested in the same way, I keep it moving. If he wants you he will let you know. Chances are if you attracted one man who had all the qualities you admire and desire then you have the ability to attract other men with those same qualities and more. When you stop settling for whatever you are offered, you can also stop blaming the men for the choices you make.

"To love someone is nothing, to be loved by someone is something, but to be loved by the one you love is everything..."

~Bill Russell~

Chapter 6

Good Intentions Gone Bad

I want you to stop and think about your last relationship that went sour. Does the scene look something like this? You call up some of your girls, because you need to get out to relax and vent. While out with your well-meaning friends, the conversation starts with you telling them about your recent breakup. The discussion quickly shifts from you telling them your story, to your girls letting you know "Girl he is a fool and did not deserve you anyway," "He is a dog and you know men cannot be trusted," "You can do better," and "You are too strong for him," etc.

They are your friends, of course they mean well and want to protect you, however these type of conversations usually end up making the man the *bad guy* and you the *innocent victim*. That does not always serve you well. You have to be able to honestly look at yourself and accept the truth about who you are and what you really want in a relationship. You also must be willing to look inward at how you have contributed to not receiving what you really want.

My last pity party went something like the one above and then I woke up. While I was trying to figure out if the wine was flowing faster than my tears, I had a moment of clarity. I began to tell my girls "my part" in why my past relationships did not work.

When I first started to look inward and discuss these things with my friends, some of them thought I had lost my mind. They went off on me saying things like "girl please! I know you are not letting him off the hook" and "you better wake up" he should not have done this, that or the other. What they did not realize is that I was not condoning the "bad behavior" of these men, I had only began to recognize and accept my own part in the relationship failure. I cannot "fix" or change a man; I can only better myself.

In all honesty, people rarely break up the first time something happens. If you allow repeat patterns of something you do not like, without ever addressing it, you are just as responsible as the person you feel inflicted pain on you. The reality is that no matter how much your girls tell you that man is wrong and no good, it is never going to get to the root of what you contributed to the relationship not working.

Sometimes you are willing to put up with subpar behavior because he is fine, he treated you well (past tense) or the ever popular "I love him." You better wake up and love yourself enough to know that any man who really loves you is not going to have you questioning how he feels about you. If you try to force something to work with a man who has told you he does not want a commitment with you, who is to blame? In case that answer is not obvious, it is YOU!

You have to look deep inside yourself and *know* that you are worthy of love. If that one man that you just have to have cannot or will not give you what you want, there is a whole world of other men out there who would love the opportunity to be a part of making you happy. When you really love yourself and are happy with your life, that one man telling you that you are not the one or that he is not ready for a relationship, will not crush you. You will be happy enough and love yourself enough to know that his leaving is a blessing for the man who wants to love you the way you want to be loved. You just have to be patient to receive what you say you want and deserve, if you are ever going to get it.

I once heard a story of a group of friends who went out to eat. The entire table ordered at the same time and then the food began coming. One by one they all enjoyed their food except for one man, who became annoyed. He asked the waitress why he had not received his food and the others had. She explained that because he had a special order his would take longer. He chilled out, because that made sense. When his food came it was all he wanted and more. The bottom line is do not get jealous or upset because your friends and associates are currently in relationships. Their men could be beanie weenies and cornbread, in comparison to the lobster and filet mignon that is being prepared to perfection just for you.

Open your eyes, go out on dates and get to know lots of different men, do things you like, have fun and appreciate each other's company. I would not recommend you sleep with any of them, until you find yourself in a committed relationship. I suggest getting to know as many men as you can to determine which of them have the qualities that you desire in a partner. Then listen to your intuition, not your hormones.

"When you think everything is someone else's fault, you will suffer a lot. When you realize that everything springs only from yourself, you will learn both peace and joy."

~The Dalai Lama~

Chapter 7

Accountability

Women please understand that this book is intended to shed light on what you already likely know deep down, and that is you have to be accountable for your own actions and stop bashing men for the actions you choose to take. There are some dishonest men out there and if one of them has hurt you, that is unfortunate. Even in those cases, I am almost certain that you could look at the situation and admit that something did not feel or seem right and questions should have been asked. These questions are not meant to nag, they are meant to protect your heart.

You have a right to ask questions about a man's intentions for you and from you. The men I spoke with consistently agreed that when a woman asked about the status of a relationship or possibility of one that it does not scare or intimidate them. If they want that woman they will have that conversation. As one man stated, if he does not want to discuss the topic and consistently "side-steps" the question, you are not the woman he wants to be with whether his mouth says it or not. His actions make it pretty clear. You may want to use this opportunity to exit stage left. If you stay it is likely you will find yourself on a visit to heart break hotel.

You do not want to go looking for trouble; you do however want to be aware. You have to open your eyes and ears because when you pay attention you can tell if a man really wants to be there. When you focus on how you feel with him it is a good indicator of whether or not he is treating you the way you want to be treated. If the answer is yes fine, but when your answer is no you owe it to yourself to get out. You cannot blame the man for not treating you a certain way, people treat you the way you allow them to. You are who you are and he is who he is and if his attitude and behavior do not please you and you have mentioned it and it still does not improve, the choice is yours! You can leave it alone, and go be with someone you are happy with or you can stay and be miserable. You cannot go around blaming men because of your inability to choose to find happiness somewhere else.

"It is not only what WE do, but also what WE do not do for which WE are accountable."

~John Baptiste Molière~

Chapter 8

Too Young, Too Dumb! - The Marriage

I got married at twenty years old, against many well intended objections. As my wedding day approached, all signs screamed do not get married. Everything in me told me this was not the right man for me. On the one hand my ex-husband was a popular and handsome man and we had some good times together. On the other hand he was a womanizer, and as I would later find out, an abusive alcoholic.

While we dated, I heard the occasional rumors about him being unfaithful to me. I would let the rumors go in one ear and out the other. Having lived in relatively small towns, it stood to reason that the stories were true, since everyone knew everyone. I chose not to listen; that was not what I wanted to hear. I would rather believe he picked me and that nothing else mattered. He had enlisted in the military and had proposed to me prior to his tour overseas. We had made plans to get married and move away the following year when he returned home. When that year passed, we really did not know each other anymore, and it would have been in our best interest to back out or at the very least postpone the wedding, instead he and I pushed forward and planned a beautiful outdoor wedding.

The universe sent so many signs.

The night before the wedding I had to go to the emergency room with a sudden illness. The medicine prescribed caused extreme dizziness and I almost missed my own wedding. If that was not enough the DJ forgot her equipment and our wedding songs played out of the trunk of my brother's Mustang.

Mother Nature made a final attempt to wake me up and get me out of there; she started my period in the middle of my vows. Thank God for full wedding gowns. As soon as I said "I do" the tears began to flow. What everyone else thought meant joy, I knew symbolized thoughts that I had made one of the biggest mistakes of my life.

I had my uncertainties before the emergency room visit, with all the cheating rumors, but I had paid no attention to them because he "chose" me. I told myself, I would be married soon and all that stuff would change. Deep within, I knew better than that. He may have proposed with his mouth and even made me his wife, but his actions told me he really had not chosen me or wanted me. Once married, his actions screamed that I did not mean anything to him. If he really loved me he would not have cheated on me, broken blood vessels in my eye, or hit me while I was pregnant, to name a few. Love would have prevented him from cleaning out the bank account to buy a new car without telling me. Love does not cause intentional pain.

If I had paid attention to all the red flags and listened to my gut in the beginning, I would have never gotten married. The marriage turned out to be an epic failure. This man had a drinking problem and he physically and verbally abused me, the thing is I could have avoided it all.

I know some may think "what a shame, he broke her heart." In the past I would have agreed with that notion, however now I realize and know better. I could not even begin to claim to be a victim in my marriage. I created that chaotic mess. I knew that he drank and deep down I knew that he cheated on me; once I found out that he was abusive, I could have left immediately. Being determined to get married and travel away from my little small town, I pushed back every red flag that I saw. I moved forward contrary to what I truly knew. I had dreamt up a beautiful fairytale marriage and everything would be wonderful. One problem, the reality did not match the fantasy. He got stationed in another state and could not get housing right away. Not only did I remain stuck in my hometown, but there I was now married and still living at home with my mother.

When I visited him a few months later, for the Christmas holiday, he and I had a colossal fight about a girl whom he had labeled "just a friend." I guess I had turned that stupid sign on my forehead off by now, since I refused to believe that. I felt and knew that more than friendship existed and I could no longer ignore it. I was obviously right, because before that trip was over my then husband had pulled a gun on me to protect his right for his "friend" to go out with us on Christmas Eve. I do not know about anyone else, but I do not have a friend that deep that I am going to risk my marriage or threaten harm to my spouse for.

I had every intention to end the marriage after that, instead one of his commanding officers convinced me to see a marriage counselor. The therapist recommended abstaining from intercourse while going through counseling. He also suggested that my ex-husband refrain from consuming any alcohol while in therapy. This man literally tried to bargain with me for a beer. One night he whispers to me "If you don't tell that I have a beer, then we can have sex." I did not even want to think about him putting his hands on me, let alone having sex with him, and all I could say was "are you serious?!" I felt so unwanted and undesired. Can you imagine how it felt to have your own husband negotiate to have sex with you for a beer? Just the thought of him touching me made me want to puke.

I returned home just after New Year's fully prepared to file for a divorce. To my surprise, he came home a few months later after being discharged from the military. He asked for another chance, which I foolishly gave, partly because to be honest I did not want to hear everyone say "I told you so." I gave new meaning to the phrase "young and dumb."

Several months later, the same behavior began, he was back to the same old thing. The only difference was now I was pregnant. I thought the fights would end because surely he would not hit me while I was pregnant with his child. Humph, I was wrong!

One night he came in drunk, cursing and screaming about who knows what, and he hit me. I fell onto our then six-month old son and that was it. "All hell broke loose" that night. I grabbed a metal rod, that I had been using to put a dresser and mirror set together, and I swung it and hit him. Blood shot from his chest and I did not know what to think. I did not know how bad he was hurt, if he would bleed to death or what. Honestly at that moment I did not really care if he lived or died. What I did know was that if I stayed, one of us was going to end up dead. I knew for certain if I stayed in that marriage any longer that he would kill me or I would kill him because I no longer would remain a punching bag. Thoughts went through my mind of leaving my son without any parents and I knew without a doubt that it was past time to go. I could not put my son through that.

I vowed to never allow him or anyone else to put their hands on me in a violent manner. I harbored a lot anger, rage and hatred for a long time about the way that marriage turned out and what I believed he had done to me. It took me a while to realize that I was just as angry with myself, because he only treated me as I allowed him to. Was he wrong for hitting me? Absolutely! Was he wrong for cheating on me? Of course!

1. **Did he break my heart?** *No! I broke my own heart! He did not do anything that I did not allow him to do. I could have walked away after the very first incident, when he showed me his true nature, but I chose to stay. I wanted to believe he would change.*

2. **Was it his job to protect my heart?** *In this case since he was my husband, I would love to answer yes. It is a great idea in theory, but in reality we are all ultimately responsible for protecting our own hearts and if we see we are being mistreated, we owe it to*

ourselves to speak up about it and to leave if it continues. .

3. **Do I regret being with him?** *No. I have an amazing and handsome son that I would not trade for anything. He would not be here if not for that marriage. For that reason alone, I am eternally grateful for our union.*

4. **Did I learn a lesson?** *Yes. I learned that once you allow someone to disrespect or abuse you they will take it as a license to continue doing so until you stop it. I learned that holding onto anger at him or the situation made no sense. My anger was only hurting me and potentially my son.*

How many times do you let a man hurt you before you see it and move on from it? That answer may be different for everyone, but one truth is constant, the man is only to blame for the first time, since you are usually unaware. If a woman chooses to suffer the same abuse from the same man multiple times, she is at fault for how she is treated because she chose to stay after seeing his true nature.

When you stay in a situation like mine or similar, you are hurting yourself and making yourself the victim. I learned that holding onto anger at him or the situation did not make sense. That anger will eat you up inside. You have to set boundaries for yourself and stick to them. You have to learn to love yourself and trust yourself enough to know that you deserve to be treated with love and respect. Do not be so blinded by what you think is love or what you think you need from a man that you lose sight of yourself. You always must know what you want from life. A man can be on the journey with you, but ultimately he cannot be your life vision.

My marriage came about because he asked me to marry him, and being young I saw it as an opportunity to build our lives away from our little towns. I quit college and thought getting married would be a quick escape route and that I would finish school once I got settled away from there. I did not have the right intent and ignored all signs that he was not the right man because I just wanted to get away. Never let what you are running away from drive you towards something worse. It is not worth it!

Do not ever believe that a wedding ring and marriage will change a man. He would have needed to change prior to saying "I do" and it would have to be his choice to change. There is absolutely nothing that you can say or any action you can take to convince a man to change. If he is not willing to change on his own or he is not what you want in a man right now, you need to leave that man alone.

You may have to be alone for a while and willing to potentially kiss a few frogs before you find your prince. Just know that your prince is not hidden in the man you have to pick apart to try to shape. It is not fair to you or the man for you to try to change him into what you desire. Your job is not to find a man and mold him into what you want, your job is to be with the man who exhibits the qualities you desire. Yes there are men who will change because they love you, but please understand that is his choice to change. If you have to force the change, it will not be a long-lasting change, it will be just enough to make you feel comfortable for a little while.

People can and do change for themselves and for someone whom they feel is worth it. You have to know that you can never prove your worth to someone who does not want to see it. When we are younger we may settle for things expecting that a man will change with age. Inherent behaviors such as abuse cannot be changed overnight or with age. These changes can only occur with the proper help and his willingness to change. My prayer for any woman in an abusive relationship wanting to work things out, is to love him from a distance. If that man really loves you and wants you he will seek the help he needs. No amount of love or understanding from you is going to be enough to change a man if he does not see himself as having a problem. Please remove yourself until he gets the help that is needed. Our intuition does not lie to us, but the key is getting still and quiet long enough to hear it and not let all the other voices deceive you. Then once you hear it, obey it.

"Whatever is bringing you down, get rid of it.
When you're free your true creativity, your true self,
comes out"
~ Tina Turner~

Chapter 9

15 Years a Fool – The Awakening

I found myself in a fifteen year on again-off again situation-ship with a man that I thought ruined my life. Once I removed myself from the situation and took a long hard look at Nicole I realized that I had again broken my own heart.

By the time I was 23, I had separated from my husband and begun to see a new man who was several years older than me. He and I each had a child from previous relationships. Neither of us planned to have any more children until after marriage. I respected the fact that he knew a bit more about life than I did. My mother on the other hand had did not trust him and warned me that the relationship just may be worse than my marriage due to his age and my lack of experience. I ignored her warnings because I was young and thought I knew it all. My mother had been close to my ex-husband so I believed she was just upset about our divorce so I paid her comments no mind. My marriage had been a disaster and I felt this relationship had to be better. After all what could possibly be worse? A few months after we began dating, he told me how lucky he was to have me in his life and how much he loved me and wanted to marry me.

All went well for about a year and a half, which is when I became pregnant. He wanted me to get an abortion, which I refused. This man was absolutely furious and began to accuse me of trying to trap him. Everything changed. He began to cheat and became mentally and emotionally abusive. Apparently, this "lucky" man now saw me as a manipulative female who would do anything to keep him. This idea made no sense to me because I knew that a child had not made me stay in my marriage, nor had a child kept him and his daughter's mother together. His comments would have been funny had they not been so hurtful and far from the truth.

Our first break up came after I became pregnant with our son. I never went after him for child support. Thankfully I was blessed enough to have a job where I made enough for me and my boys to be okay. The boys and I lived with my mother for a couple of years until I was able to fully get back on my feet. He began to come visit our son. Eventually I took him back, rather than acknowledging that he could not or would not give me what I truly wanted; A real relationship with love and commitment. My mother again had warned me not to go back to him, as she saw straight through him. By now I was in my mid-twenties and still too hard headed to listen to my mother's advice. In my mind, she just wanted to "be in my business." You know how we are quick to put people "in our business", until they tell us something we do not want to hear.

I moved to St. Louis and rented an apartment when the boys were entering kindergarten and second grade. My plan was to buy a house before I was thirty-five whether I was married or not, as long as the kids were in a good school district and I liked the area. My youngest son visited his dad on alternating weekends. I did not like that arrangement since he was living with his ex-girlfriend's grandmother and there were lots of problems. Once I became settled into my apartment his dad moved in with us. Things were cool for a little while.

I suggested he and I purchase a small affordable investment property to restore and rent for additional income. Each day after work, I would go to the property to work with him; knocking down walls, hanging drywall, and mudding and taping. I had no reservations about the work because it would be an investment in our future, or so I thought. A few months into the house project I began to get really sick. I thought I had the flu or a sinus infection and I went to the doctor, who prescribed me an antibiotic. Two weeks later, I was still sick and went in for a follow-up visit. The doctor told me that I was eight weeks pregnant. Looks like I would be having the "flu" for another seven months. This pregnancy caught me off guard, since I was now in my early thirties and my sons were school age. Though it came as a surprise, it was a pleasant one for me, I love my sons and I knew I would love this baby also.

I decided that this was as good a time as any to buy my house, thirty-five was only a couple of years away and besides the additional space would be needed for the baby. He was enraged when he found out I was pregnant and adamant about not purchasing a house. Again I was accused of being deceitful. He made it clear that he planned to leave and he argued that we could not afford another child. He moved into the unfinished property, determined not to provide any financial support. I chose to have my daughter despite his decision. The more I thought about it, it became clearer that he had not been a contributing factor to my household, merely an occupant.

I did buy my house, and it was a beautiful 3 bedroom brick house, vaulted ceilings, arched doorways, and a huge backyard where I put a pool for the kids. The large basement had a foosball table and a pool table for the boys. My main attraction was the living room, it had a big beautiful fireplace encased with a gorgeous built in bookshelf. I would sit there curled up on the couch for hours and read. My sons especially loved having their own space to be kids.

Once I had my daughter, their dad began to lurk around. One day, unexpectedly, that lonely woman syndrome crept in and somehow I had let him convince me that I should move into the investment property with him to save money for a larger home and to get married. I gave up all I had and moved into this trial sized house in the hopes to marry someone who had already told me and shown me so many times that I meant less than zero to him. Two years later we still lived in that little house, still had not gotten married and truthfully still could not stand each other. Resentment grew and bitterness set in.

I did not come from a wealthy family and I never considered myself pretentious, but I believe I should provide a good home for my children in a safe environment. I had aspired to have so much more from life and to provide my children with better opportunities. We had two very different life philosophies, and somehow I had lost myself in an attempt to please him. When I would mention striving for more, he would retort, that I thought I was The Queen of England and other snide comments. That is when I began to see that his subtle and not so subtle insults over the years had chipped away at my self-esteem and made me question my worth and whether I wanted too much. I had begun to question whether or not I really deserved what I wanted. I cannot recall exactly when I had lost my mind and given him control over my life, but obviously I had. I had given this man nearly all my twenties and thirties before I woke up to the realization that this insanity had to end, I had to leave.

I had tried to recreate the relationship we had at the start, rather than the reality we now lived. I lost self-esteem, friendships, and my sanity. The worst part is that my children were not afforded a truly stable and healthy childhood. I had become a mess and had been so desperate to have a man that I lost myself. I had somehow became one of those women who feared being alone. I had been insulted and dejected by him so much that in my mind he was the only man who would want me with 3 kids. This caused me to go back time and time again. Each time a little more Nicole was lost. The fear that another man would not want me caused me to settle for the lowest treatment from someone who clearly did not deserve me. While I knew that I had seriously jacked up my life up to this point, it took my then sixteen year old son's words for me to truly open my eyes. My son voiced something that I already knew and had not wanted to admit "mom if he has not married you in fifteen years, he is not

71

going to." Although I knew it, to hear my child say it to me was so embarrassing, I could no longer ignore the facts.

I began preparing to leave and my mother took ill. I became paralyzed at the thought of losing her and I stayed a few months longer, however her death caused me to take action. Sunday June 24, 2012, I stood over my mother's casket for a final goodbye. One of my friends said to me, "I have not seen you in years." That is when it hit me like a ton of bricks; a light bulb came on and it all became crystal clear. I had unintentionally alienated myself from my friends and family just because they detested him. It was well past time to move on. I knew without any doubt that I was done for good.

I thank God for the plan he had in motion. My inner voice had gotten its shout back and I began to listen to it. My brother called to gripe that his tenants had messed up his house and had moved without warning. I could not have been happier if Ed McMahon and the Prize Patrol were at my door; in my mind all I heard was "Cha Ching, I'm moving!" I told him not to rent to anyone else, that I wanted to move in ASAP. He warned me that the previous tenants had left the house disgusting. I walked into old wet mattresses and trash bags in the middle of the living room, filthy bedrooms and a bathroom too hard to describe. My initial thought "No way am I living here" but just as quickly as that thought came, it vanished and the vision entered.

I got a vision of how the house would look once it was cleaned and had my furniture in it. I left and went to the store and stocked up on cleaning supplies and gallon jugs of water. I knew that I would have to do a deep clean once the water and electricity were on, but in the meantime the gallon jugs would have to do. I needed it to be bearable for me to get in there and clean those old items out. I wasted no time, I worked the entire weekend and through the holiday to get the house ready. For the first time in a long time I knew exactly what I wanted and I could not afford to miss the opportunity. I had been through enough and was determined that nothing would stop me from moving. I moved out over Labor Day weekend and never looked back.

Though I struggled for quite a while to get settled, I pushed through because I had to get it together for my children. My bad judgment had made them the real victims. Whatever struggles I encountered or would have to face could not even begin to equate to the peace and freedom I felt knowing we were completely done. The hard work was worth it, it signified FREEDOM! I began to realize that I never needed him because I had been my family's own provider the entire time.

Somewhere through all that mess, my life changed, I had been fooled to believe the mental and emotional lies that I got from him, messages that said I should give more, do more and be more. I had stopped being my own cheerleader in an attempt to boost his ego. The problem with that is that I gave until I had become a dry vessel, and rather than help me refill he just picked at me until I cracked. He had no intent to marry me. He had nothing to offer me, but somehow I had been convinced that I needed him around. I had told myself the kids needed to have a man around. Then I began to realize that having a man around should not be the goal. The goal is to have a healthy household where the kids were free to move around; free to have friends over; free to live comfortably and just be kids. I had fallen for the misconception that a piece of a man was better than no man at all, which just is not the case.

If you do not know what desperate looks like, the above scenario is your blueprint. Apparently I had been so thirsty for marriage that I had lost all good judgment. Somewhere along the way I had allowed him to knock me so low that I believed myself unworthy. You have to be careful about the men you allow in your life and in your spirit. It started with all the wonderful compliments. Then here and there came the insults or jokes that were meant to be funny, but felt hurtful to me. It had gotten to the point that insults came as frequently as the compliments. I had not paid attention to the fact that as my spirit was weakened, I had permitted him to make me feel small. I questioned my worth more and more. I had bought into the idea that I could do no better. The mind games built me up, just to knock me down. I had allowed him to build his self-esteem at my expense.

It took me a lot of years to wake up from that foggy relationship, but when I did I knew I would never go back. A good man, a confident man, will build you up, because he knows that the higher he builds you as his woman, the higher you both will go. He will not insult you or try to hurt your heart. He views you as his partner and his equal. He will be your biggest fan, not your competitor. That is the man you want in your corner.

Some may call me stupid and say that there is no way that you would have stayed or made the decisions that I made. Some may be in a similar situation or have been and you think about how hard it will be to get out. Whatever thoughts you may have are fine if you get the message behind the story; and that is, never lose yourself trying to hold onto a man.

The irony is that when I went into the relationship I had high self-esteem and loved myself unconditionally. I affirmed him and expressed to him his value to me and as a result, he felt the need to tear me down. His actions spoke so clearly that I was not "the one." I however chose to pretend not to see that. If you are in or have been in a similar situation, please know that you are worth all that you desire. Let go of any limiting belief that you have to be in a relationship to make it. Get clear and laser focused on how to love yourself.

Mental and emotional abuse can create long-term scars that must be addressed. You must be open to reach out for help if you need it. You are not alone. The mind is what controls the course your life takes, and if your mind is not clear your whole life will be chaotic. I am taking my time and learning who I am and loving me again. There is not a man alive worth giving up your entire life for.

I would be in a terrible place if I had not sat down and got real with myself about what had happened. I spoke to counselors, read books about abuse and talked to friends about how I felt. I no longer feared what my friends and family would think about me for repeatedly going back to him. Instead I accepted that I had made mistakes and I owned them grew and am still growing from them.

That man told me he had no desire to have more children and when I got pregnant he showed me that he meant it when he gave no support for them. When I looked at the entire truth, I could not be mad at him because we had not married, he had shown me that he had not planned to marry me after my first pregnancy. I still chose to go back time after time. I could not even remain upset that he provided no financial help. I made the choice to lay down and have unprotected sex with this man and continue to be with him again even though I knew how he had reacted after our first child.

I learned a hard lesson, but it made me stronger. I could begrudge him for not supporting our kids, but who would that help? Resentment would not pay the bills. When I left I had to go through a process to heal. A process to forgive. I first had to forgive myself and accept that I had allowed myself to be treated so poorly. Once I forgave myself it became easy to forgive him. I realized that he had told me he wanted to marry me but he had also said that he did not want any more children before marriage. If I am honest with myself I realized that once I got pregnant the whole relationship changed. I broke my own heart time and time again in that relationship. I disregarded the big picture at the start of the relationship. If I had left after his initial reaction to the first pregnancy I could have saved myself from years of heartache and pain. Instead, I chose to believe he would change, since he came back I thought I would get what I wanted.

Sometimes you try so hard to listen for a man's words to tell you that you are not the one, that you do not pay attention to his actions that show you that you are not "the one". I knew deep down that a marriage between us would not happen, but I did not want to be alone. I have since grown and know that it is better to be alone and happy than in a relationship and miserable. Men are quick to claim a woman that they want. That same man got married three years later to a woman he begin dating after I left.

If a man has not claimed you in a reasonable amount of time it is because he does not value you or find you all that important in his life. You have to set boundaries and not empty yourself out for others. Every time a man cheats on you, lies to you or belittles you and you accept it, you show him that you believe you are not worth his respect. Please stand up for yourselves and do not allow yourself to be disrespected. No one should get the opportunity to make you feel that you are less than great.

1. **Did he break my heart?** *No. I have to take responsibility for my actions. I admit that I had doubts about the relationship after our son's birth. I had played the on again, off again game too many times with him. I was not forced to stay or go back. Those were my choices.*

2. **Was it his job to protect my heart?** *No. That is always going to be my job. Listen to your intuition and pay attention to how you are treated. Don't let anyone make you feel like a victim. RECLAIM your POWER!*

3. **Do I regret being with him?** *No. I have a wonderful son and daughter as a result of that time together. For that I will always be grateful. I live with no regrets only lessons learned.*

4. **Did I learn a lesson?** *Absolutely. Never lose myself trying to keep or find a man. I also learned that mine only becomes ours after the marriage. Never again will I give up everything on a promise.*

I lost a lot and had to take baby steps, but I learned that baby steps are fine, as long as I stay in forward motion. It has taken me some time to re-establish my worth, rebuild my self-esteem and to let go of the garbage that I allowed myself to believe. I still face challenges, but I would not change Labor Day 2012 for anything in the world. That is the day I reclaimed the woman that I know I am meant to be; the woman that I am becoming. I refuse to let anyone make me feel like I am less than God's very best. I will no longer accept the lies that I deserve less than I desire to have. The dreams and goals that I once set aside are born again and more alive in my soul than ever before. I was born to shine, and shine I will!

"No Weapon formed against me shall prosper, I am more than a conqueror" Isaiah 54:17 (Holy Bible)

Chapter 10

Separated is Not Divorced

Another scenario where I should have known heartbreak would be imminent was the case of the separated man. I have definite rules about not getting involved with a married man. Of course everyone knows single available men are fair game. However, I did not have one single rule regarding separated men, those going through a divorce. I had never put much thought into it because the situation had never arisen. As I got older, I encountered more men who were on the verge of a divorce, and since everyone has a story, who am I to judge? When separated men began to approach me, I had not taken into consideration the fact that separated is not the same as single. I had not previously been interested in any of them who had approached me; so it really had not mattered.

When you do not have rules, you tend to learn as you go, and learn I did. I learned the hard way that separated men merit their own rules and boundaries that differ from those for single men. A man who is in the process of dissolving a marriage, and who lives in different house from his wife may seem like fair game, but think again. That is not always the case. You may tend to give the separated man a pass that you would not begin to give the average single man. Somehow these actions seem logical and understandable at the time.

Say you begin spending time with a single man, a few months pass and he says to you "babe we can't go out tonight because she will get upset"

What would you say? Be honest! What would your initial reaction be?

I would be willing to bet money that a lot of you would want to know who "she" is and why "she" is more important than you. You would probably begin to envision what the other woman looks like, her social status, when she came in the picture, and why it matters if she sees you. You may even tell that man off and leave him standing there as you strut off, simply because he was bold enough to tell you that "she will get upset."

Take a similar situation with the separated man. You two have been kicking it for a while and he tells you "baby I would love to take you out, I want to show you off to the world, but baby if she finds out I am seeing somebody I can lose it all."

How would you respond? What would your reaction be? Would he get the same treatment as the single man?

The separated man would probably get a pass because you assume "she" is his wife. You would perhaps get all compassionate and envision him on skid row; no house, no car, no job, bye to the kids and poof the two dogs are gone. You may even become extra sympathetic to this man and hand out passes like candy at a Thanksgiving Day parade. Why? Because God knows you would hate to be responsible for him "losing it all." For that alone, you may buy into his story - hook, line, and sinker, not once even considering that "she" just might be another woman other than his estranged wife. It may never occur to you that he could be twisting his words just right to keep you where he wants you. After all, you do not want to rock the boat by asking any questions, right? Wrong!

Newsflash, you better wake up and start asking questions. If you do not ask questions and that boat sinks, it is likely taking your heart under with it and you have no one to blame except yourself. You cannot afford to assume you know the answers to unasked questions. I learned from experience and watching men and talking to men that more often than not, separated men use lines like those above to keep women at bay while he does whatever he wants to do. A few sweet lines and compliments and it is a done deal.

When I left a fifteen year relationship, I had no clue how to go about dating again. To say that I was socially challenged would be a major understatement. Many things had changed since I had last dated and as a result my ego took many bumps and bruises. One of the biggest bruises came from dating a man who was going through a divorce.

It all came about innocently enough. One day while busy at work, I decided to take a break and check my social media account. A message notification flashed, alerting me of a new inbox. This message was from a man who I had fallen for years earlier, asking me to call him if I wanted. My initial instinct was to ignore the message, since things had not ended well between us. The last I had heard he was happily married and I had no intention of being a side chick. A few days later, instead of leaving well enough alone, my curiosity got the better of me and I called him.

The man on the other end did not sound like the strong, confident man that I remembered, in fact the man on the other end of the line, sounded flustered and discombobulated. I heard a baby crying in the background, and thought I had misdialed. After it was confirmed that I had the right number, I asked about the baby. He explained that he had custody of his son and that he was going through a divorce.

I had no intention of starting anything back up with this man other than the friendship that he so desperately sounded like he needed. He and I begin to talk on the phone a few nights a week, but I was not sure just yet how I felt about seeing him face to face. Since I was coming out of a long term "situation"- ship and he was going through a divorce, it had been agreed that a relationship was not in our best interest. After a few months of phone calls, we finally decided to meet up and see a movie. Once the movie was over, we went back to his house and talked and caught up on what was new for each of us. Quite some time later we eventually became intimate and were seeing each other at least a couple of days a week and just about every other weekend. If I was not at his house, he was at mine. I had met his best friend, he had introduced me to his kids and he knew mine. We spent our birthdays and the holidays together. If this man would go out on the weekend, he would call and check-in. Keep in mind I had not asked him to do any of that. Things seemed to be going along smoothly, or so I thought.

At no point up to here had he mentioned having changed his mind and wanting a relationship, I just assumed that we were in a relationship because it had started to feel like one. It felt like a relationship, it looked like a relationship, it must be a relationship, right? Wrong!

Reality hit, the day I asked him about going out for the evening and he told me he would not feel comfortable going out as long as he was still married. That is when it hit me like a ton of bricks, separated is not the same as single. I had not taken the opportunity to ask two very important questions, "Do you even want this divorce?", "Have you had a change of heart about being in a relationship with me?"

I thought I knew the answers without asking the questions. Never assume that you know anything without asking. No matter how good or bad the answer may be, you have to ask the question. Ignorance is not a defense. If you want to be able to make an informed decision, you must ask the necessary questions. After several months passed, there was no mention of how the divorce proceedings were coming along. I was beginning to wonder if there would be a divorce. It seemed to me that though his wife was physically in another house, she still occupied a huge portion of his mind.

Within weeks of my request to go out, a "friend" of his from the military and her sister came to town and stayed with him for about a week. In this week that she was in town, my timeline had begun to flood with a myriad of photos of the three of them and his and her kids with fun poses and smiling faces, horse drawn carriage rides, visits to museums and local monuments all over the city. It was clear that they were enjoying their time together, and he had not looked the least bit uncomfortable. I felt like a damn fool, I was livid! In my mind, I thought "how dare he take her out and do all of these things and not be willing to go out with me." He rationalized that his wife knew this woman because she was a long-time friend of his and that spending time with her would not cause any legalities with his wife. Somehow, I had been pulled back in by that explanation, and still had not asked the necessary questions. I had not addressed the issue of whether or not he was now ready for a relationship, and if so did he want it with me. I had gotten lost in the words that he had given while explaining their "friendship." I soon noticed, that he still made excuses for not taking me out and I, like a fool, had accepted them. This man and I continued spending time together, until a month before his divorce was finalized. He ended things telling me that I was not whole and complete and that I needed to heal from my past relationship.

A couple of months after the divorce was final, pictures of him and a young woman begin to surface on social media. They were cuddled up at concerts and grinning from ear to ear at restaurants and just the picture perfect couple. In fact so picture perfect, that it was evident that they had not just begun seeing each other. Turns out she had been a woman that he expressed interest in while seeing me. It soon became crystal clear that I was the placeholder he needed until his divorce was final.

The majority of men I talked with, agreed that the first woman they dealt with after their divorce, was temporary, a bed warmer, a rebound, a placeholder, whatever term you prefer to use does not matter. What does matter is that if you settle for being that woman, the man is not likely to choose to settle down with or marry you. Unfortunately whatever the reason, it does not ease the pain. If he tells you he is not ready, believe he is not ready and move on if you want more.

No matter what anyone says separated is still married, and most men are not about to go from one marriage directly to another. If you are ready for a real relationship or desire to get married, my suggestion to minimize heartbreak, would be to leave that separated man alone until after the divorce. He is not likely to jump from the frying pan into the fire again anytime soon. Give him time to get himself together and decide if he is ready for a relationship. If you are still available when or if that time comes you will be able to decide if he is someone you want to spend time with, without the games and drama of a looming divorce. No matter how great you may be, you will not be good enough for that man who just is not ready or who is not interested in you.

Love yourself enough to know that if he wants you he will pursue you once the divorce is final, but do not just wait around for him to make all the rules. No matter how you slice it separated is still married and the situation can get complicated. You cannot be led solely by your emotions. You have to balance listening to what he is telling you, while at the same time watching what he is showing you. The two should be in alignment, if they are not you need to start asking questions so that you are armed with the right information to make knowledgeable decisions. Then you have to be brave enough to walk away if you are not getting what you want.

1. **Did he break my heart?** *No. The reality is that I broke my own heart. My heart got broke because I opted to ignore my inner voice that said he is still legally married and you deserve better. Rather than quiet myself and listen to my own intuition, I chose to look outside of myself for love. He did not break my heart. He only treated me how I allowed him to treat me.*

2. **Was it his job to protect my heart?** *No. I know right from wrong and I put myself in a compromising situation, therefore I have to be adult enough to take*

accountability for the consequences of my actions. I knew I would eventually want a relationship and that could not happen with another woman's husband, separated is not divorced.

3. **Do I regret being with him?** *No. Life is too short for regrets! I cannot change the past only learn from it.*

4. **Did I learn a lesson?** *Yes. I had been angrier with myself more than with him because I had lied and pretended to myself that I was in a relationship that did not exist. The truth is I had chosen to stay through all the drama, even though that man had told me he did not want a relationship. I saw what I wanted to see. I could have walked away at any given moment.*

Women, you have to stop giving your power away and then playing the victim. I now affirm myself daily and I have since resolved that if a man is not helping me advance in my life, he has no say in my life. When you know your value, other people's opinions of you do not matter. Love yourself, appreciate who you are and celebrate you. When you do these things you become so strong inside that you will no longer be willing to settle for anything less than the best.

"The most common way people give up their power is by thinking they don't have any"

~Alice Walker~

Chapter 11

Playing With Fire

The sun was shining and it was a crisp breeze blowing, an absolutely gorgeous day which was rare for the end of October. Rare and perfect since it was my 40th birthday weekend!

I had just left the gym and was about to drop off my son at the barbershop. I had planned to head home and get ready for my night out. This would be the day that I saw this fine man, who I recognized from one of my social media accounts. He and I had never met, but have quite a few mutual friends. Thank goodness he did not see me. Usually I would be digging my new look and confident enough to approach him. Not today! Keep in mind I had just left the gym. I had done the big chop on my hair and ditched the creamy crack a few months earlier, and my TWA (teeny weeny afro) did not look too fly after the workout and sweat. I was rocking a fuzzy sweaty little afro, my natural looked super-natural. The last thing I was about to do was introduce myself.

So the chicken in me waited about a half hour and then I messaged him to ask if it was even him. It was. He looked better in person, so I was unsure. He inquired as to why I had not spoken. Of course I could not tell the man that I had just come from the gym and my hair looked a hot mess. I opted for the other truthful answer "you were on the phone, and I did not want to bother you." I let him know that I would speak next time I saw him to which he responded, "Please do!" We exchanged messages over the next few days, and then I decided to ask the question, "Are you single?" My instincts had told me that a man as fine, funny, charming and sexy as he was, would probably not be single, but I did not want to assume.

His first response, "that's a tough question" really said it all and should have been warning enough. It was not! I countered "no not really, it is just a simple yes or no." The second response, "I'm single as in not married, but I do have a friend that I've been seeing for a minute" should have sent me running for cover to protect my heart. It did not! He mentioned that she lived out of state, which should not have made a difference to me, however it did. I reasoned with myself that it could not be too deep, or she would be here with him. I ignored the fact that since he mentioned her at all she must have meant something. While I appreciated his honesty, why had I even asked the question, if I was not going to respect the answer? Instead of respecting myself, him and his "friend", I played jeopardy and decided to flirt. By continuing on, I was basically saying "is that your final answer?" I knew deep down I should have stopped flirting and left well enough alone, but I could not see past what I wanted.

The following week, I conveniently found myself at a Halloween party where he was. As I entered the party I ran into an old co-worker who I had not seen in a long time. The co-worker leaned down to give me a hug, and just as he let go, "Mr. Single with a friend" approached me. He grabbed me and gave me this really tight hug as he whispered in my ear "you told me you would speak next time you saw me." Now normally I do not hug strangers, but this man's arms did not feel strange. I did not want to let go.

He was working, so we only had a few brief exchanges throughout the night and flirted here and there. He asked me what I was doing after the party, and invited me over to his house. I initially said no. We exchanged numbers, but just before leaving he invited me to another club. We talked and slow-danced until that club closed. After all the closeness of slow dancing, I have to admit going home was the last thing on my mind, however, my friends and I left the club. Just a few minutes later he called and asked where I had disappeared to. I was just a bit up the road from the club when he told me that he was at a gas station close by and asked if I would meet him there to talk for a minute. We talked for a little while until I realized how silly we looked hanging around at the gas station so late and I was about to go. Again he invited me over to his place.

I surprised myself the way I snapped letting him know that nothing would happen. It had been just a little more than a year since I had been with a man. I had taken the last break up as time to work on myself and had not realized it had been so long. I actually thought it had only been a few months until I started calculating. It had been so long since a man had held me like he had when we danced, that it made me unsure of where things may go that night. That is when the realization hit. I had not snapped because I did not trust him, I snapped because I did not trust myself.

He took no issue with the fact that there would only be conversation. He and I talked and just cuddled until falling asleep. I woke up a few hours later face to face, with his arms wrapped tightly around me. Unfortunately, I had to work later that morning on an overtime project, which meant I had to go. What I really wanted to do was lay there and keep breathing in this man. I felt more than comfortable, I felt safe. As I was leaving he gave me a t-shirt to cover my costume and he walked me out. I thanked him for being a gentleman and headed home to get ready for work.

I was unsure if or when I would hear from him again. I was surprised when I got his text later that evening, asking what I was doing. He invited me over and said that he had been debating going to a friend's party. I could not leave seeing how I had just picked up a girlfriend of mine and arrived at another girlfriend's house for a bonfire. I could tell he was trying to tempt me to leave because he and I texted back and forth for a while and he reminded me of how cold it was supposed to get that night and mentioned that he knew I had to be cold out there. I thought it was cute and as much as I would have loved to be cuddled up in his arms somewhere, instead of freezing every inch of my behind off, I could not just leave my girls hanging.

A couple of days after the bonfire I called to see if he wanted his shirt back. Lame? I know, but I was trying to justify a visit. He said yes that I could bring it over after work. I teased him when I got there and told him I was leaving since he had his shirt back. That is when he admitted that he did not care about the shirt and just wanted to see me. Although I did not admit it, I am sure he knew that I had used the t-shirt as an excuse to see him also. In an attempt to keep my feelings at bay considering his situation I would not invite him to my place. I thought that would keep me from getting too comfortable. I was wrong. We ended up seeing each other on several more occasions before we eventually became intimate. He and I started to see each other a little more frequently over the next few months. This man was funny, caring and considerate of my feelings. He listened to me and responded without judgments about me. I really enjoyed our time together. I had gotten comfortable and felt safe falling asleep and waking up in his arms. That is when I knew I was in trouble. I can count on one hand the number of men I have been intimate with, and I do not easily get comfortable with men this quickly. I got scared because now that light bulb came on, the one that reminded me that I was falling in love with someone else's man.

How in the heck did I let that happen?

Short answer - I had played with fire! Now I was about to get burned.

When I started to realize I had fallen in love with him, I had to tell him. I needed to know if he had any feelings for me. I knew if I went any further without me finding out how he felt, that my heart could be shattered. What I did not know is that I had already waited too long. I had already fallen knee deep in love with this man and heartbreak lurked around the corner.

One night we had a disagreement about something he suspected I had done or would do. I did not appreciate how he talked to me and I did not like how things ended that night. A couple of days later, after work, I went over to his house to discuss it. When I told him how I felt about what had happened the previous night, he hugged me and told me not to hold things in that it would make me sick. He encouraged me to always tell him how I felt. So in my brilliant mind, I decided to express to him that I had developed feelings for him. He asked almost sympathetically, "Why? You knew my situation." I had to try to pretend that question did not sting. Up to that point, he had always been so attentive to me when we were together, that I had honestly forgotten about his "situation".

He was not mean or spiteful when he asked "Why?" he just seemed genuinely confused about it. That question stung, because I knew it was not just a question, it was more of a declaration and a reminder of what he and I were not. Whether genuine confusion or not, about why I had come to feel the way I did, did not matter. What did matter is that he had already told me that there was someone else in the picture. I had no reason to be mad at him, and not just because I had fallen in love with him, but because he had not done anything to me. He had been upfront about there being someone else.

I had asked the right questions, but chose to ignore the answers. I learned that no matter how charming, kind, handsome, funny or sexy a man is, I owe it to myself to say "You're cool, holler at me when or if you don't have someone else." You have to learn to believe a man when he tells you what he wants or does not want. When given the information to make educated decisions, you cannot make heart felt and emotionally driven choices; when you do, you set yourself up for failure.

I can write about this now and realize that at the time I did not value myself enough to believe I could have a real relationship of my own with a single, handsome, kind, caring and good man. I took what he offered knowing that he said there was someone else. I could not get mad at him because I had pursued him. Honestly at one point I chose not to believe that he really had someone else. Since we were messaging online, before we met, I thought just maybe, he thought I was "catfishing" him and had made the other "situation" up to limit how close I could get to him in case he saw me and was not interested. Can you say delusional?

I am glad though for the experience; it opened my eyes to remember who I am and to know and believe in myself enough to never settle for being less than #1 ever again. He saw that I was willing to play second best, and he let me. I know there may be someone saying "he knew exactly what he was doing" and, or "that is what she gets" both could be true, nevertheless neither of us are bad people. We are human and we made a bad judgment call.

I have always been that woman to look sideways at other women who messed with someone else's man. I never thought I would be her. I tried to justify it to myself by saying, he said she is a friend; he has only been seeing her for a little while; he does not sound too sure because at first he did not even want to acknowledge her. I ignored the voice that said she must mean something or he would not have brought her up. I had tried to justify things just because I wanted to be with him. You can never say what you will or will not do, because you just may get put to the test.

1. **Did he break my heart?** *No! I broke my own heart. I could have chosen to walk away before I ever let things*

get that far. I could have stopped messaging him as soon as he told me about his "friend", but I did not.

2. **Was it his job to protect my heart?** *Of course not! He is not obligated to protect my heart. He was straight up with me and I chose not to listen. I wanted what I wanted and ignored my intuition. That inner voice said "Nicole do not do it, he is telling you that there is someone else, do not go after someone else's man" I did not listen and I hurt myself. Guarding my heart is my job, I was given the necessary information to do so and I chose not to.*

3. **Do I regret being with him?** *No. I enjoyed our time together and besides life is too short for regrets! I cannot change the past only learn and grow from it.*

4. **Did I learn a lesson?** *Yes. I learned I am too good to be less than any man's #1 priority and that by accepting anything less is damaging to my own self-esteem and will cause a man to de-value me as well. I also learned that when a man tells you that there is someone else, it does not matter if she is across the street or across the country, if he acknowledges her that is where his heart is and that is to be respected.*

I knew better, period! I had forgotten how it felt when it happened to me, and I warranted it by saying "well, I have been cheated on before and the other women did not care about me." Whatever justification you can come up with is not worth the heartache and headache you are likely to feel later. No matter how much fun and excitement you may foresee, no matter how much he may flirt and no matter how attractive he is, if you are looking for real love, you cannot find it with someone else's man. Do not find yourself heartbroken and crying in a pint of Haagen-Dazs. Just Do Not Do It! If you do it, you may not be like me and fall in love with the man; you may end up the unfortunate woman to later have your man cheat on you. KARMA is REAL!

I believe that man cared about me. He just could not love me like I wanted and needed to be loved, and that caused me to change how I responded to him. I want and need a man that is mine, a man who chooses to make me a priority, a man willing to grow and build with me, and a man who acknowledges me as his woman. I need a man who openly and honestly communicates with me, treats me well on a consistent basis and cannot wait to hold me, kiss me and make love to me regularly. I need a man who knows I can stimulate his mind, body and soul as long as he is my man alone. At that point, neither of us could be that for each other because he belonged to someone else. I can admit to still loving him, but I knew that as long as he did not feel the same way about me there would be no future there.

If you put all your heart into loving someone where there is no future then you will never get the love you truly desire and deserve. I am not saying you can instantly turn off your feelings. I am saying be careful of the situations that you allow yourself to get into that have the potential to hurt you.

"We accept the love we think we deserve"

~ Stephen Chbosky ~

Chapter 12

It's all in the Approach

I am a confident woman when it comes to men. In the past if I saw a man that I was interested in, I had no problem making that known; however over the years, I have learned to set some boundaries. The relationships where I initiated contact with the man turned out okay, but ultimately they did not advance to the level I would have liked them to. I learned that when a man is truly interested in a woman, he WILL approach her and pursue her. There is no such thing as he is too shy, he is going through a lot right now, he is intimidated by you or whatever other line that you may be telling yourself. If a man REALLY wants you, he WILL make sure you know.

A little bit of flirting in the form of smiling and making eye contact is usually enough to bring a man over to you, if he is really interested. Once you laugh and smile to get his attention and to let him know that you are attracted to him, he can see that you are a friendly and approachable woman. If he is interested in you at all, you will not have to do much more than that for him to initiate contact and spark up a conversation. When you flirt and are aware that a man has noticed you, be patient, give him an opportunity to come to you. If he does not approach you or return the flirtatious gestures, it is usually a clear indication that he is just not that interested in you. Do not take it personal; it could be that he is married, otherwise involved with someone or maybe the hard truth really is you are just not his type.

The good news is that there are other men out there who are available and whose type you are. You do not want that man who you have flirted with early in the evening who has ignored you all night, but then comes around near closing, after he has put on his "liquor goggles" and every other woman he tried to get with is gone or has given him no play. Who wants to "win" by default or as a last resort?

Don't you want a man who will want you back?

I found that the relationships where I initiated contact, and pursued the man eventually progressed into me initiating all aspects of the relationship. It did not feel good. It got exhausting putting in all the effort. It felt like they were on auto-pilot and just going through the motions. I do not know about you ladies, but I want a man to desire me and to want me. When I stopped putting in all the effort in those past relationships, the men would inquire as to what was wrong with me, never acknowledging their part. You know why? They had become accustomed to me "running the relationship," and why not, I had done it since day one. In the beginning of those relationships, I had messed up the male and female balance that I had longed for. By the time I felt that something was wrong, it was too late, and they were not willing to do any more than they had initially been expected to.

I have since learned to show a man interest and let him pursue me if he is interested. When a man wants you, he has no problem putting in the work to be with you. You have to set your boundaries before a relationship is developed so that you are prepared to deal with the relationship that you create.

Do not sell yourself short, you are worth being pursued. The only men who do not think so are the ones who are not meant for you. Don't you want a man who is willing to take the initiative to be with you, a man who appreciates you and values you? I am not saying to never take initiative once in a relationship, but let the man be the man and show you that he really desires to be with you and wants to protect and provide for you. You are worth that and so much more.

"Never let a man tell you twice
that he doesn't want you"

~Judge Lynn Toler~

Conclusion

You cannot close yourself off from the possibility of love, you have to be confident that real love will come and although you cannot guarantee which relationship will be the one, you can control what situations you involve yourself in to maximize your chance for true love and happiness.

You have to take into consideration, not just that a man may love you, but that he loves you the way you need to be loved. You cannot blame a man for not fulfilling your fantasy of a house, white picket fence, three kids and a dog when he has already told you he does not see a future with you. It is not your responsibility to make a man what you want him to be. He has a right to want something different; it is your job to be brave and patient in dating until the man who wants the same thing as you do comes along. Quit trying to change these men; either accept the man he is or leave him because he deserves to be happy in the relationship also. Although every relationship I have been in is not included in this book, I did look at all my relationships and each one had an element to learn from. I am asking you to learn from my mistakes, and to please do not break your own heart and hurt yourself.

As I write this book, I can say that I truly love myself and have healed from my past hurts and forgiven perceived wrongs of the past. I have accepted the part I played in failed relationships and I own my mistakes and learned from them. I know that I am no one's victim. I take full accountability for my choices. I now choose to only allow single, available men to have my time. I love myself enough to know that the man who is truly meant for me will be single, available, and attentive to my needs; He will love the beautiful, strong, outspoken woman that I am and will gladly make me a priority and not an option in his life.

I often hear people say that someone loved them past their pain, and that may be true. Love yourself first and not leave that job solely to the next relationship partner. I learned to love myself past my pain because I do not feel that it is fair to make the next man pay for mistakes I made with any prior man. Be aware of how you have contributed to failed relationships. Accept that you made some mistakes and learn from them. Be accountable for taking care of your own heart. Let AAA take you confidently into your next relationship. Awareness, Acceptance, and Accountability.

"If you focus on results, you will never change. If you focus on change, you will get results."

~ Jack Dixon~

34293240R00061

Made in the USA
Middletown, DE
17 August 2016